PEARLESQUE

ADDITIONAL WORKS

HAVE NINE LIVES

Poetry: Published By: Cykxbooks 2021
A collection of poetry that delves into the depths of the human experience, capturing the fleeting beauty of love, loss, and rebirth. Through each verse, discover the resilience of the spirit and the quiet power of transformation.
"In the spaces between lives, we find our truest selves."
ISBN (Paperback): 978-0-932436-31-3
ISBN (Ebook): 978-0-932436-74-0
Available at: www.bowerybooksandsarts.etsy.com

PEARLESQUE

Tristan Buttigieg

MCMLXXVIII

CYKXBOOKS

New York ~ New Hope

PEARLESQUE

Copyright © Front Cover Images and Design by Tristan Buttigieg
Library of Congress Control Number: 2024951590
ISBN 978-0-932436-33-7 (Paperback Edition)
ISBN 978-0-932436-76-4 (Ebook Edition)

Published in the United States by Cykxbooks,
An imprint of Cykxbooks Publishers.
Cykx and associated logos are Trademarks and/or Registered Trademarks in the US Patent and Trademark Office and other countries. Marcas Registratas of Cykxincorp.

CYKXBOOKS
A Division of Cykxincorp,
P.O. Box 299
Lenox Hill Sta,
New York, NY 10021
cykxbooks@cykxincorp.com

Manufactured in the United States of America
1 2 3 4 5 6 CBP 26 25 24 23 22 21

CONTENTS

In this collection, the words are brought to life by the poetry that speaks to the heart, and the images that evoke the mind. These are their interpretations.

HECTIC ELECTRIC BRAIN DRAIN

Roaming fields of discordian toasters are excellent actors.

The same piece of paper goes through the looking glass.

The count-down of numbers goes faster & faster.

Until we see what the masses...

Are up to now.

Amid the windows are the bisexual characters & symbols.

Stuck between barriers less than one inch away.

The ripened bar grows larger, and the cookies will crumble.

You can clean all your actions by using the risk name...

They gave you.

Fifty-eight minutes with a two-hour ordeal.

Power among power is to be erased by the hour.

Sleep-deprived eyes weren't part of the deal.

The running of the television, and the silence of the tower.

Leave your mouth gaping open a half-baked face.

The snake's hiss is growing louder, and it's stuck inside the
box

Choose now what insert should be jammed in its liver.

Orange eyes are dreaming and in sync with the clocks.

While your head bangs on the desk becomes bigger.

But what the hell do I know, right?

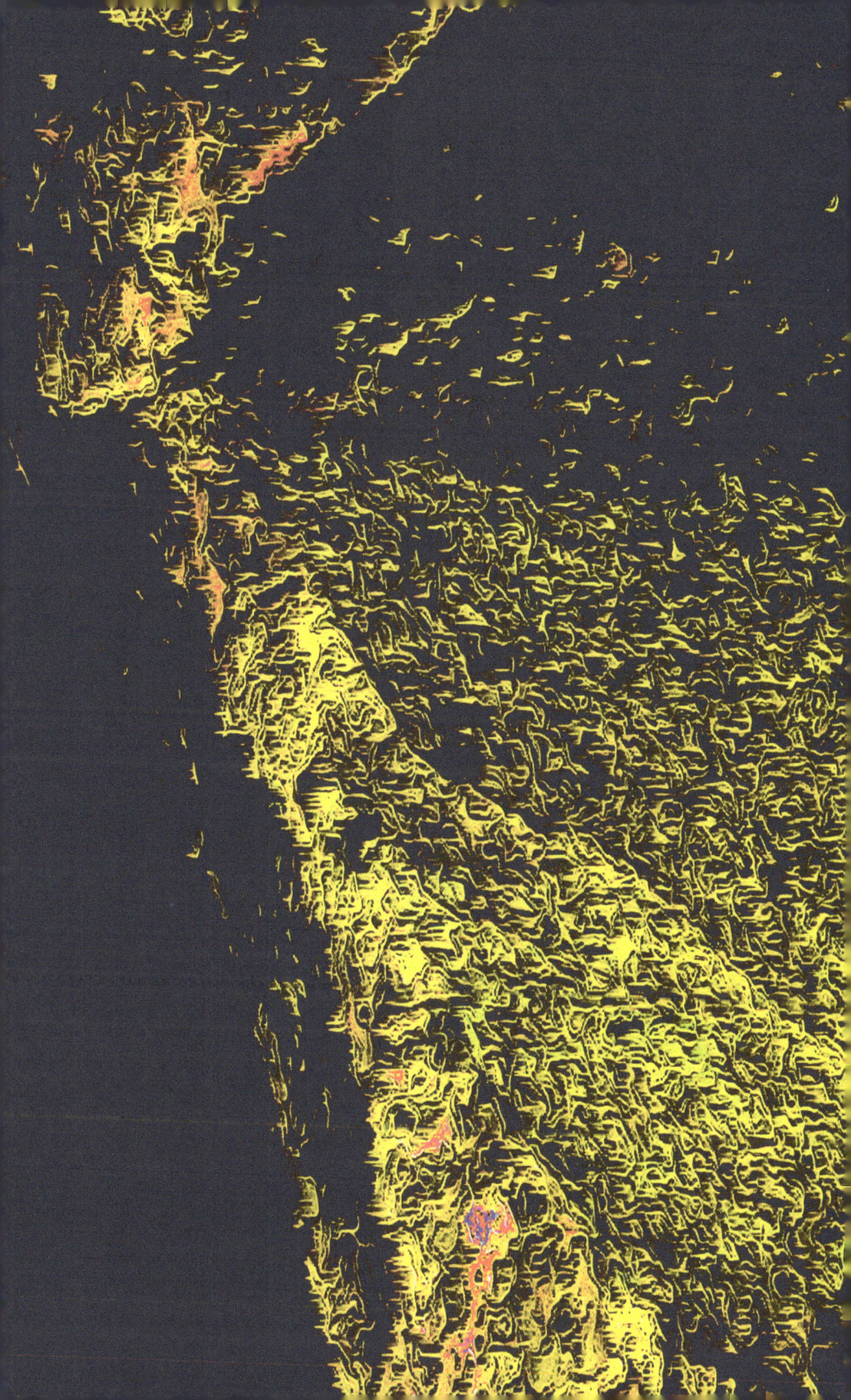

COPPER QUEEN

Beauty of a woman sitting still on the rocks

Races come charging like a flock of birds

Lead me with your light that's made of gold

And persuade me to stay with your green-tinted body

Tell me the good, the bad, the ugly, the pretty

Embedded in the lines of your constructed face

Tell me the history, the marks, the overall fantasy

Of living in a world that's different from mine

Show me the hustle & bustle, the sweet sounds of a lake

Tell me who lives here, from dull grey to dark green

I have so many questions for my Copper Queen.

The eyes of the goddess are windows to the future

The broken pieces are memories of the unmarked past

And to think it was made for a silly like me.

Lend me your wisdom, your guidance, your lust for knowledge.

Towering the world, what do you see?

A standing stone, are you ever alone?

Elemental battle, do you have the strength for it?

Do you feel like an animal, caged in a zoo?

Admired by most, but never appreciated?

A symbol of freedom or just a common theme?

I have so many questions for my Copper Queen.

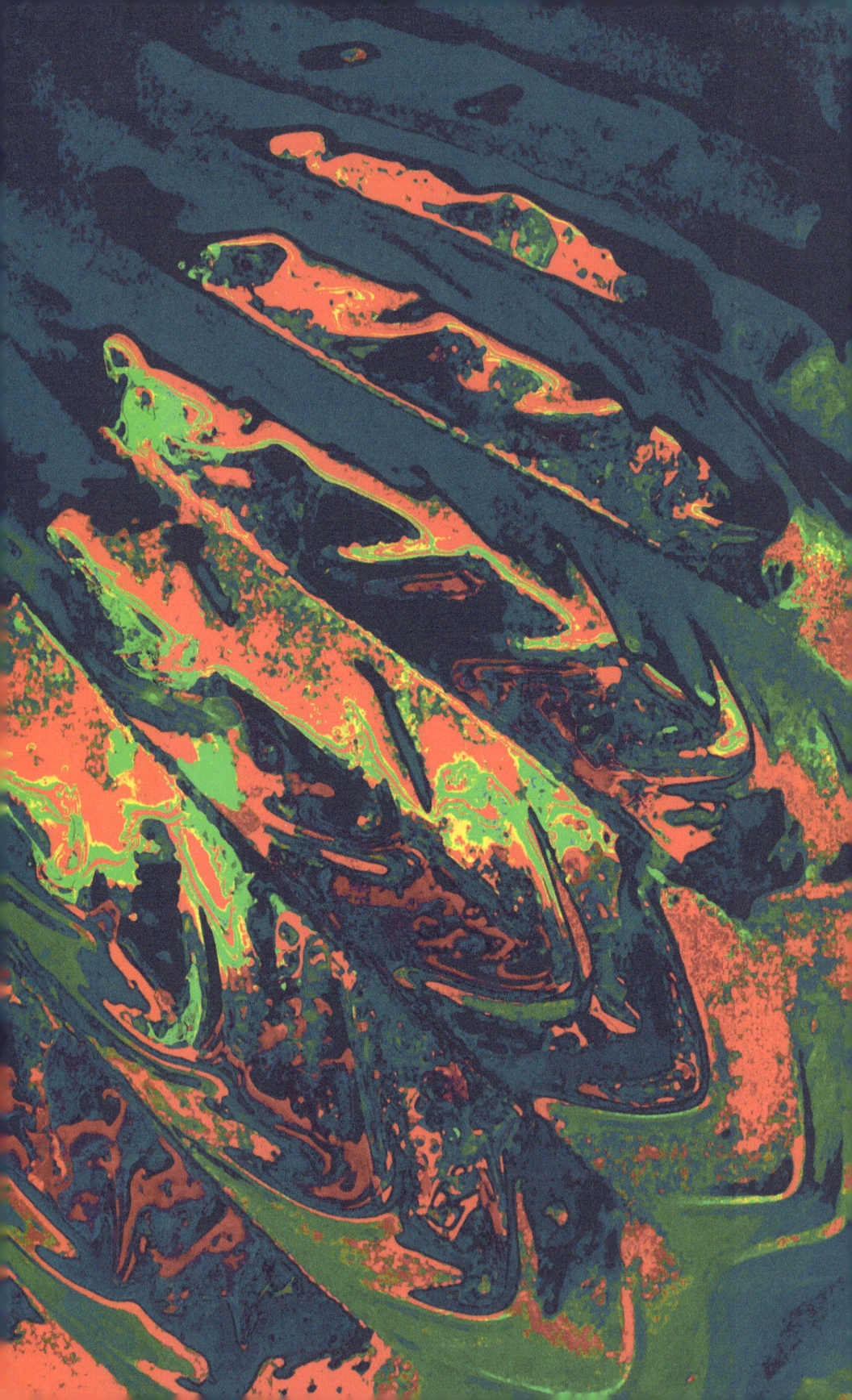

YELLOW MICKEY

Ripped it enough
Took it only for the night
Dripping lips
Spoken in tongues
Surrounded shrines
Where do you bury your dead?
Rolling whistles
Cryptic texts
Born to the core
Designated whipping posts
Pressed against the weight of the lights
Fashioned desserts
Flailing rain
Shrunken through the lenses
Religiously on the same page
Dripping
Whistling seven more houses
Playing it tough
Washed awake, are you blind?
The hours passing fancy
Soaring hands weighed away
Seventh heaven
For the first tear
What starts a life for all?
Same sparks in the race
Smashed their tongues in the water
Raised a long crashing show

Breaking news
Her hands shaking to the rhythms

PUPPET MASTER

An innocence in your eyes
Was it before or after?
Outmatched
God sent
Please go on
While I continue to drop

Top scarecrow props
Spreading the bubbles
The glass cocoon fights
The apple orchards throughout the city
In vain
Two twins reduced to names
Fearing the misses will see

Usual orders
Extendible mouths
The blind leading the blind
Shattered
Slanted
The curtain drops
Cold winter blows
Left from last time

LE HAVEN

Real as the rooms
A night saved from the shame
One-stop
The hot seat
The limitation of the day
What smut
The live bait
A jerk flowing downstream
Damn the torpedoes
We"ll watch the fireworks

The flock of old souls
A frenzied rip in the sky
Death currents
New spirits
A candid crypt in the scenic light
Big talker
Free agent
Flying in a fevered swim
Damn the torpedoes
We'll watch the fireworks

The lines of a lie
The half-hearted strapped in naked frames
The older shades
Decided on what part of the heart it hits
Second run

The slimy heels
All went soaring with the smoke
Damn the torpedoes
We'll watch the fireworks

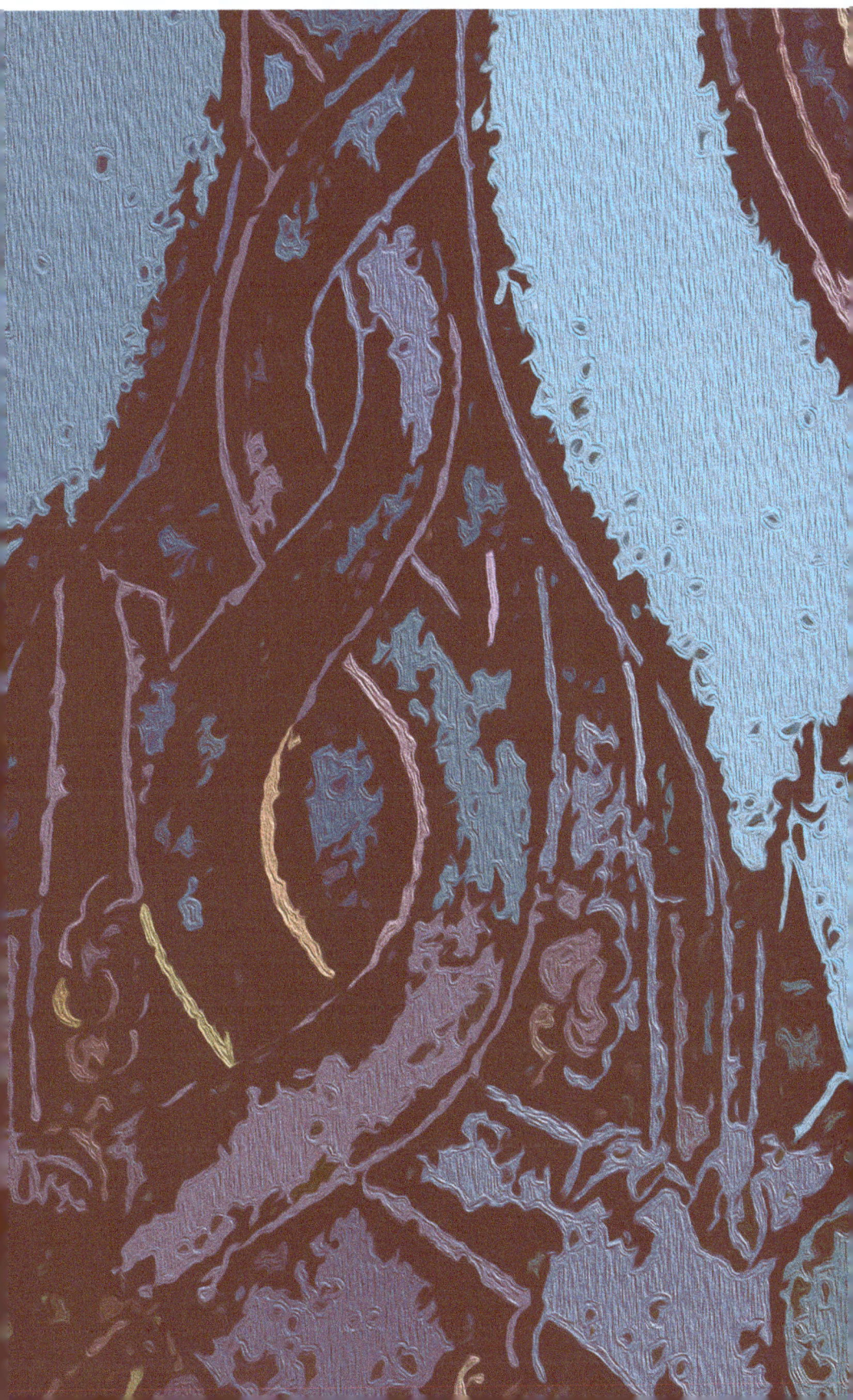

ILL GOTTEN GAINS

Gave up the ghost
The stately portraits in the sun
Stony glow
An old horse
The photographic waves
Standing naked on the road
Sub Rosa
Hard knocks
The several vicious stops
No thrills
The flower yards
The mark of the dead
The undeveloped soul
Sweet treats
A stunt cake
All the blood rushed through their heads
Sudden death
A scratch off
You got caught red-handed ma'am
The scars of a genius
New scenes
And old start
The disemboweled order
Water-run
Straps off
All the weapons up their sleeves
Kicked their high heels off

Comfort zones
The crooked parts
Cooked it and made it cry
Steeple points
The rusted knees
Keep on whistling, I'm still alive
A wounded animal that never wins
What do they fall like?

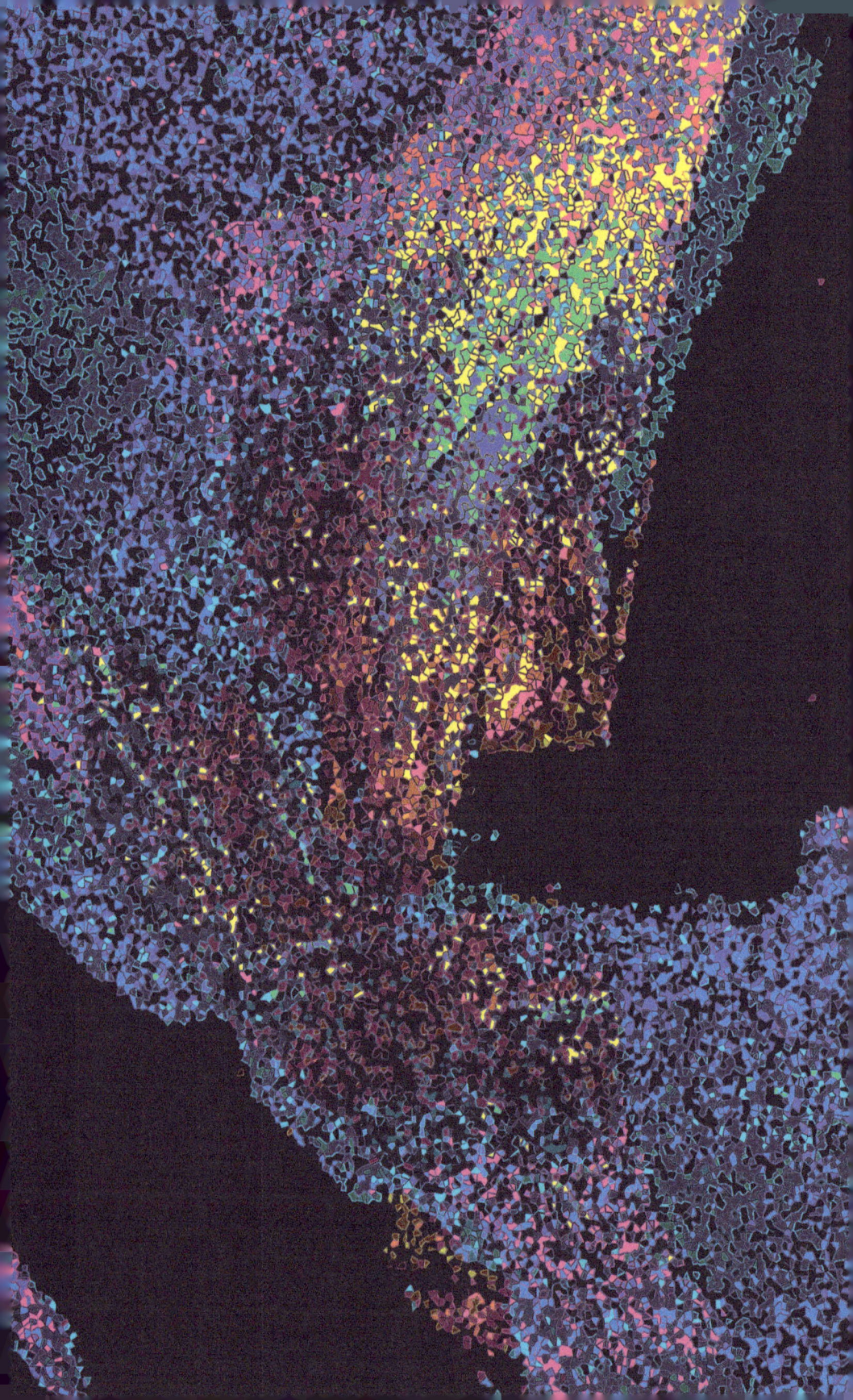

DEAD CAT BOUNCE

Sounding like a couple of rogues
A peppered scheme in synch with the wreck
Hunched a roll
A pair of thieves
The angry strokes of snow
The sounds of cabaret follow
Funny girl
What a way to go
Passing his final stop at the beat
The saint living near his house
Strewed petals
Stained plates
The thrashing scores across his face
The absent color in her eyes
Crouched tigers
No survivors
Flops a freeze of feathered planes
Where were you when the lights turned out?
Drink the dregs
The unarmed resistance
Watching them flutter as they skimp in their stalls
Stacked with shadows
The scattered remains
The desolate plot of splattered lines
Calling cards
A stairway to the stars
Milky white scores across their arms

A sign of the despots
The classy little actress
Splattered sparks in a jumping dance
The flailing scores in the sea
Can't die from that kiddie
Watching them run with the crown

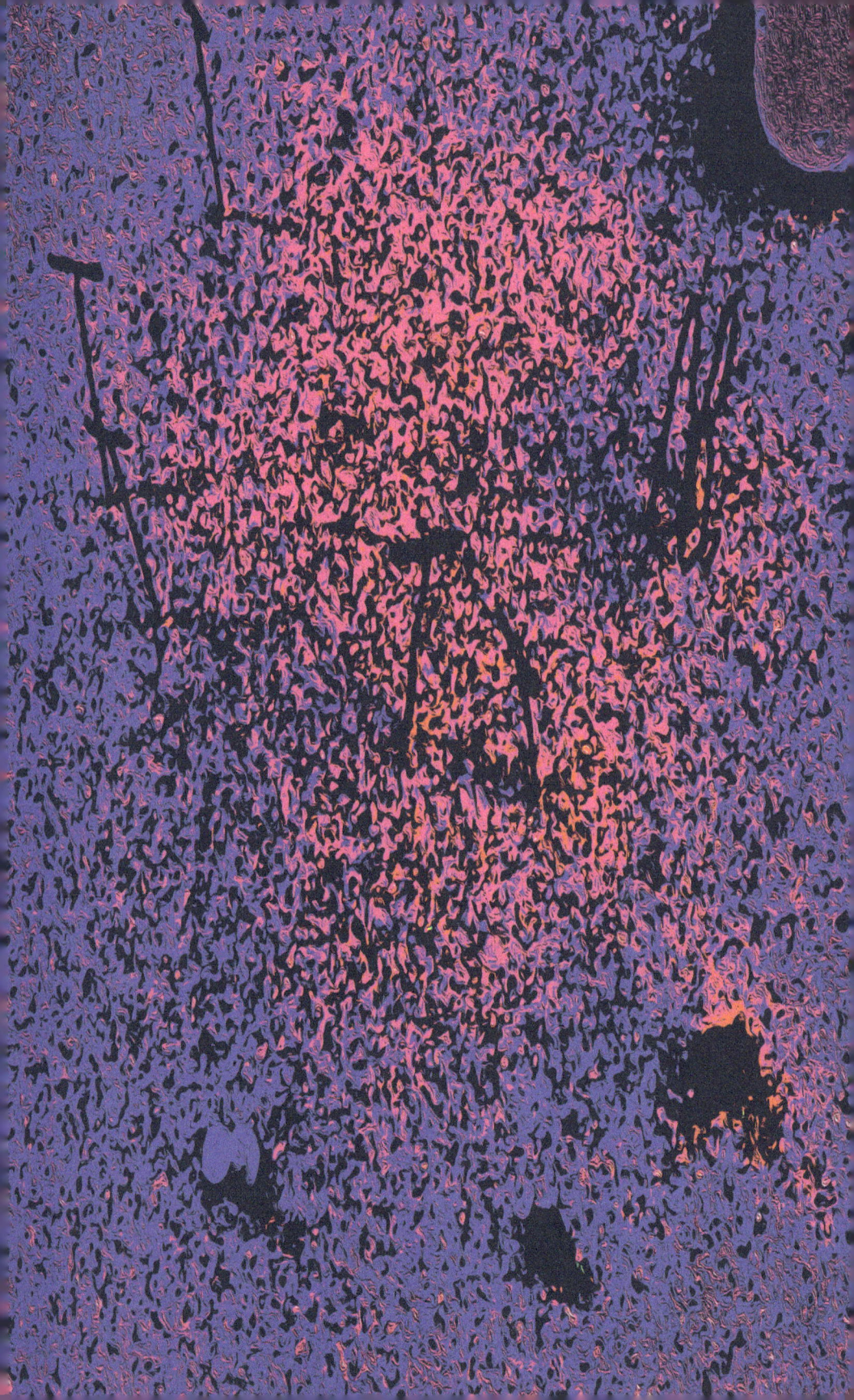

ROGUE'S GALLERY

Booked a brave face
They just sit there and stand
Dearly departed
The shredded sea
Leave them for the crows
They're born in snow globes
New scenes
Old hearts
A disintegrated sky
Showered dreams
The great divide
The mightiest touch
A piercing moon divided by light
The drops of a salted crest
The misconducted step
They roll the sidewalks in at night
Scrolled like a book
The embarkment at the board
Stick to the script
The scars on their skin
Molded faces in a swaggered bird dance
Raising their hands to the sick
A stream of stars
The calibrated shards
Jagged notes in the slits of her dress
The opposite attraction of her flailing ghost
She sent me a stunner

Imagine all the clouds they must touch

CAPELLI MILLINER & TAX-XITA

Cappelli Milliner

Flashback to Brooklyn in New York City
Walking the streets in your bottomless shoes
The mangled streets, boxcars, and Model T's
The sidewalk stores, went away one by one
The polluted sky, a factory for our disease
Walking in the streets of a once happy place

Flashback to the tenements for immigrants
Coming home from work at the age of nine
A family of ten, eight kids with the same name
Just to make a penny, to keep them all alive
A few arms were cut, was all a numbers game
Coming back home of a once-happy family

Flashback to find the difference in every block
It wasn't the clothes, or the protested child laws
It was not roaring, like this little world of mine
It was the hats, where it gave them some identity
Swinging the thought of an impossible dream

Fast-forward ten years to when I became a man
Decided to walk to California with hopeful intentions
Wrapped my belongings in some polka-dot dresses
Mama cried in my thought of leaving
Daddy said I need to work on the machines
But they knew this was no place to live

Fast-forward seven months to the flats on Melrose Avenue
I've magically completed my journey, and I kiss the ground
for comfort
But I didn't have any money, so I served as a slave
Went back home in my box-sized deluxe
Ate all the food that I found in the trash
Waiting for the rain to wash my clothes
But this was a dream come true for me

Fast forward two weeks with my last day on the job
The torture was hard, and the pickings were rough
The gate opens, and in comes walking artistry
Wearing colors that I thought were mythical
Blue eyes piercing the heart of my soul
Had glistening hair, not the rugged type
But she looked familiar in some way or another

Fast forward one year to Dallas in the state of Texas
I landed a job that was better than the last
Shucking corn, until my hands turn red
Hoeing the ground in perfect little lines
Still had my dream of opening my store
But I knew that it would take some time

Fast-forward to the home that I've built myself
Lives my family, a wife, three kids, a mule
Acres of farmland for as far as I can see

Clouds so puffy you could sleep on them
You can't beat this anywhere kiddy

Still currently living in the countryside
I saved enough money on the side for myself
I saved enough money to open my store
Of selling hats, like the ones back home
Of selling identities, in the only way I know

One year later, after some negotiation
I plan on going back to Hollywood, California
I left my wife, taking the kids along with her
She took the wagon, and I at least took the mule
Too much violence, too many altercations
She was not a compatible partner, really got in my head
I knew that this was a sign from above

During the same year in the Hollywood lights
I opened my store that's now become a reality
In my dreams of connecting with people
Not a very big store, but it will do
At least the rent every month is cheap
Cause it was more than what I bargained for

Ten years later, down on the boulevard
The business is growing, with many types of hats
Fedoras, Turbans, Skimmers, and Berets
For men, women, or for any creature

For a while, I was one of the few stores selling hats
But then there was competition brewing

Currently, in the twenty-first century
The business has fallen on some hard times

Hats have become a thing of the past
And now cell phones are the latest fad
I can only imagine how the store across is doing

Currently, in the twenty-first century
I had to sell the business for profit
Went back to my box-shaped luxury
Now in quotations, but it's all I got
I'm reliving my past all over again

Currently in the twenty-first century
I feared my life would be over soon
No way to eat, no shelter to sleep
I can't even afford the thread to make hats
Did I just make a terrible mistake?

Tax Xita
Flashback to 5th Ave & E 76th St, in Manhattan
Walking the streets in your high heel shoes
The pleasant parks, love, and affairs in the air
The sidewalk stores, anything that you want
The crisp clean air, a cigarette blown in there
Walking in the streets of a once perished place

Flashback to the house that was built just for me
Coming back home from play at the age of five

A family of four, eight cats with the same name
Just to take a penny, to keep myself happy
A few dollars spent was all a numbers game

Coming back home to a slap-happy family

Flashback to find the difference in every flat
It wasn't the clothes, or shopping for gold
It was not boring, like this little world of mine
It was the umbrellas, to remind them of pain
Twirling my hair of a doable dream come true

Fast-forward ten years to where I've grown bored of this
life
Hopped on a plane, to reach for fame
Mama said just don't get robbed by men
Daddy said we'll just hire the lawyer
But they really wanted me out of the house

Fast-forward seven months, chock-full of hissy fits
It took some time, to get my suite on Melrose
Avenue
I had all the money, and hired a slave
Went to the mall to buy out the store
Ate all the food that was prepared for me
Got what I wanted with a snap of a finger
But I'm just living a life like before

Fast-forward two weeks to when I ran out of money
I open the gate, and that slave's just staring at me
Wearing clothes that I thought were scorched
Had rugged hair, not the glistening type
Grey eyes that make me want to vomit every time
But he looked familiar in some way or another

Fast-forward one year to Dallas in the state of
Texas
Asked daddy for money during that time, then he cut me out
of the deal
I knew it would only last so long
So, I landed a job making actual money
A strip pole tease, giving guys the night of their lives
Still had that dream of opening my store
But I knew that it would take some time

Back then in the apartment that I rented with others
I live with my lovers, a wife, and three men
Acres of bad boys, and the boots in the package
Pumping out the fetishes, and drowning in dollars
People who just can't be richer than me
You can't beat this anywhere baby

Still living my life on the cityside
I stole money from my lovers without them
knowing
I now had enough to finally open my store
Of selling umbrellas, like the ones back home
Of selling sorrow, to my smaller subjects

But the neighborhood was just too violent

Day by night, I'm somehow still breathing in the
city
I'm upset that my recent endeavors turned to stone
My lovers left me, with the money taken away

They figured out my schemes, but I don't care
Too much pleasure, not enough attention

It was just too easy, no pain in the process
I knew that it was a sign from above

Fast forward ten years later, in the Hollywood lights
I racked up enough dough until I called it quits
I slept with a mixture of fat cats, skinny dogs, and rats
Then I wasn't needed anymore down in the big D
Now that the younger girls have replaced me
But I reopened my store which was now a reality
After some negotiations, and some favors on the side
Keeping my dream alive of making people
wounded
A very big store, but it will do
At least the neighborhood isn't as violent as the last

Ten years later, down on the boulevard
Growing the business, many types of umbrellas
Polka-dots, stripes, curved and straight
For men, woman, or any clown
But there was competition brewing

Currently, in this new-aged race
The business has fallen on some hard times
Umbrellas have become a thing of the past
And now the rain has just been accepted
I can only imagine how the hat store across is
doing

Currently, in this new-aged race
I had to sell the business for profit
Reluctantly asked my dad to lend me some money
But even him, the bank, has no money as well
Not in exclamation, but I'm a little upset
I'm living a hell that could not be dreamt

Currently in this new-aged race
I feared my love would be over soon
No way to buy, and no way to gloat
I can't even afford those high-heeled shoes
Did I just make a terrible mistake?

NICK O'TIME

Tanks in exclamation
The excess blood in their words
Brew ha-ha
A crash in the clouds
The methods of her touch
The merriment of youthful chases
Wishful woes
Rapid roads leathered in their hair
Sunken planes
Ledges of the sun in the layered smoke
Putzing in his yellow raincoat
Pins & needles
The scattered battle lines
Calling cards
The broken blush
Handwritten bashings on the walls
Bloodied breeze
A stream of sange in the sapphire
Rose to tragedy
The valley between people
The debonair of a sunless highway
Fight or flight
Broken light
In honor of the young
The pink corollas tattooed on their guns
It's not a dream child.
The movements of a nightmare

Called them by the roadside
There's no distractions at the bottom of the river

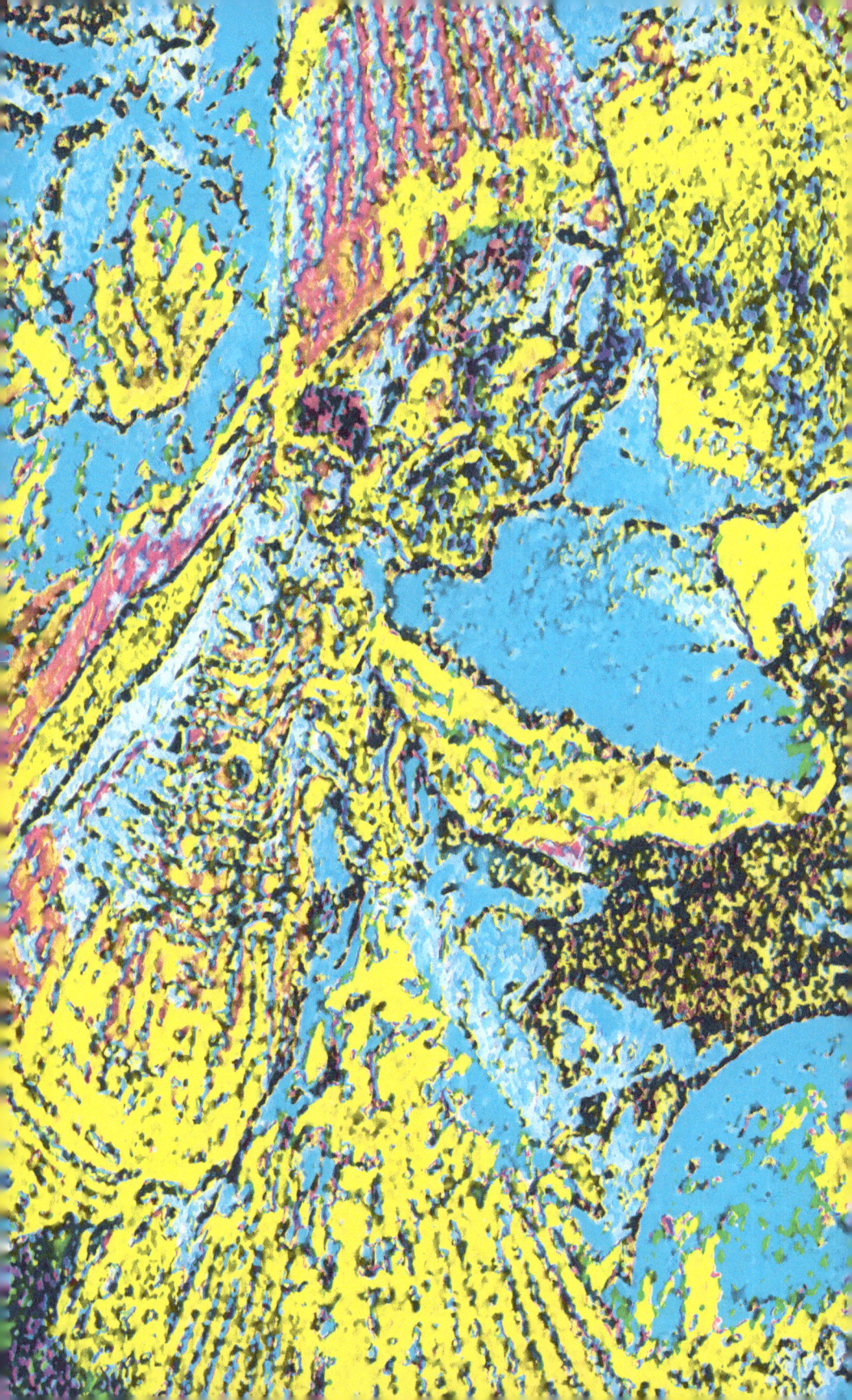

RED SAVINA

Inventions of the woven
The crush in their cursed sets
Piss poor
You cause an uproar
May they turn to stone
The arrested vex on the web
Sweeping cries
Foiled gags
The barking call of formed hysterics
As they watch the streets turn to ash
Farewell
Forlorn
A splattered script of a bloodied beach
The final vestige of the free
Dumb, buoyed a look of rotten teeth
Stumped the plunge
The sad climb of slaves
Caked a charm of auburn skies
As they watch the streets turn to wine
Needle-nosed jerk
The rips in their sleeves
The shaped lip of a naked disguise
As they watch the streets turn sour
Oh, what invention!
The acrobatics of the departed
Ashen-faced
The running bleach in their eyes

All the steady stokes
As they watch the streets turn to grease
The show must go on

DRESSED TO THE NINES

Laugh clown laugh
The partial list of the dead
Boohoo
Damaged roots
A stand-alone post in the arms of the damned
Pale acclaim
The crumbs of the crash
Tired eyes
A stickered mist
Hurricanes in their hearts
The tight rope cadence
Can dance the speckled shake
Button-up
The will & whim
The earliest wave
A polished grin
The splattered stars on their thighs
Hearts in their eyes
The unpredicted curse
A break-off boulevard collapsed in the stretch
The interwoven specs
Hot & heavy
The silk of her skin
An echoed glow in a shaded disguise
The peaceful calm of their shredded news-stands
Sing me a new one
The scattered cloak of their jumps

A devil in disguise
The sounds of a diluted noble
The swallowed bloat of the tunnel
Pardon me yutz
Crusty cracks on the streets
Do you expect this to keep clean?
Blurred cash
The zig-zag commotion
A penny shock on every block
The bunched crimps on the screen
It's looking like Halloween in the hills
Don't forget we're all still animals.

FOLIE A DEUX

Graded waves sign the scene
The fashioned wince of an ominous crash
Newcomers
Lone rangers
The convenience of society
Tough crowd
Darkness roars on fainted shores
Hummed a buzz of crescent blare
Charmed & tragic
The speckled smooch
Hush, hush, honey
The guilty conscious
The masquerade in the charring heat
In a scam-footed retreat
Oh, what the bleep!
The bastard cracked his hands
Posture & pose
Fallen shadows
The heated glow of a high-horse esteem
Those wicked schemes
Stony hands
The beating hearts
A slouched content
In their rummaged brains

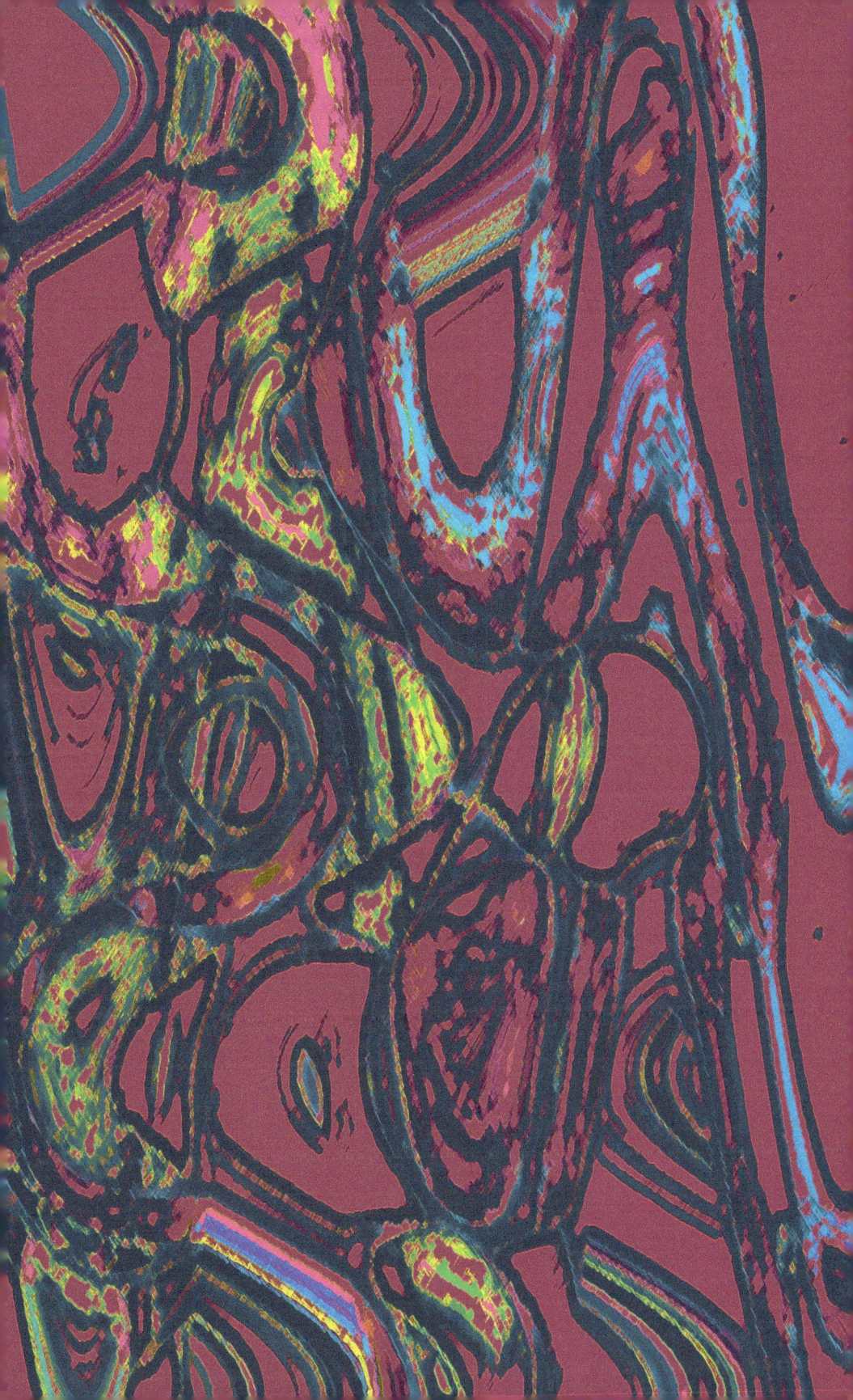

HOBO STACKS

Came and went with a new rule
Trial by fire
The hungered plight of sunlight
Spoiled noise
The sudden stop
The hurtled mass of speed-bump speech
A wonder shot of whittled teeth
A swift retreat
The birds with no flock
Lucky shot
A wounded smile
Oh, go jump in a lake
Surrounded by the silence of sound
Crashed ashore
The grit in their kiss
Cut of the cloth
The tsunami in her dress
Vague by the side of pale tidings
The sad score of doves
Shooting star
The twist in your kiss
Sunny days
You can see their smiles grow loose
The suspenseful wait
A birthday bash for the brave
A crooked swan dance
The evidence all over your face

Quiet chants
The polished shine
The spades and hearts of traveled beats
Blades of rain parachute the street
Double dreams
A loud retreat
The razored pleats of casket screens
Running down the smiles of thieves
Plummeting down the hillside
Hunger strikes
The ready stokes
An encounter in his flirtatious skirt
Blushing in the sweat of the rain
Do they have to go so far?

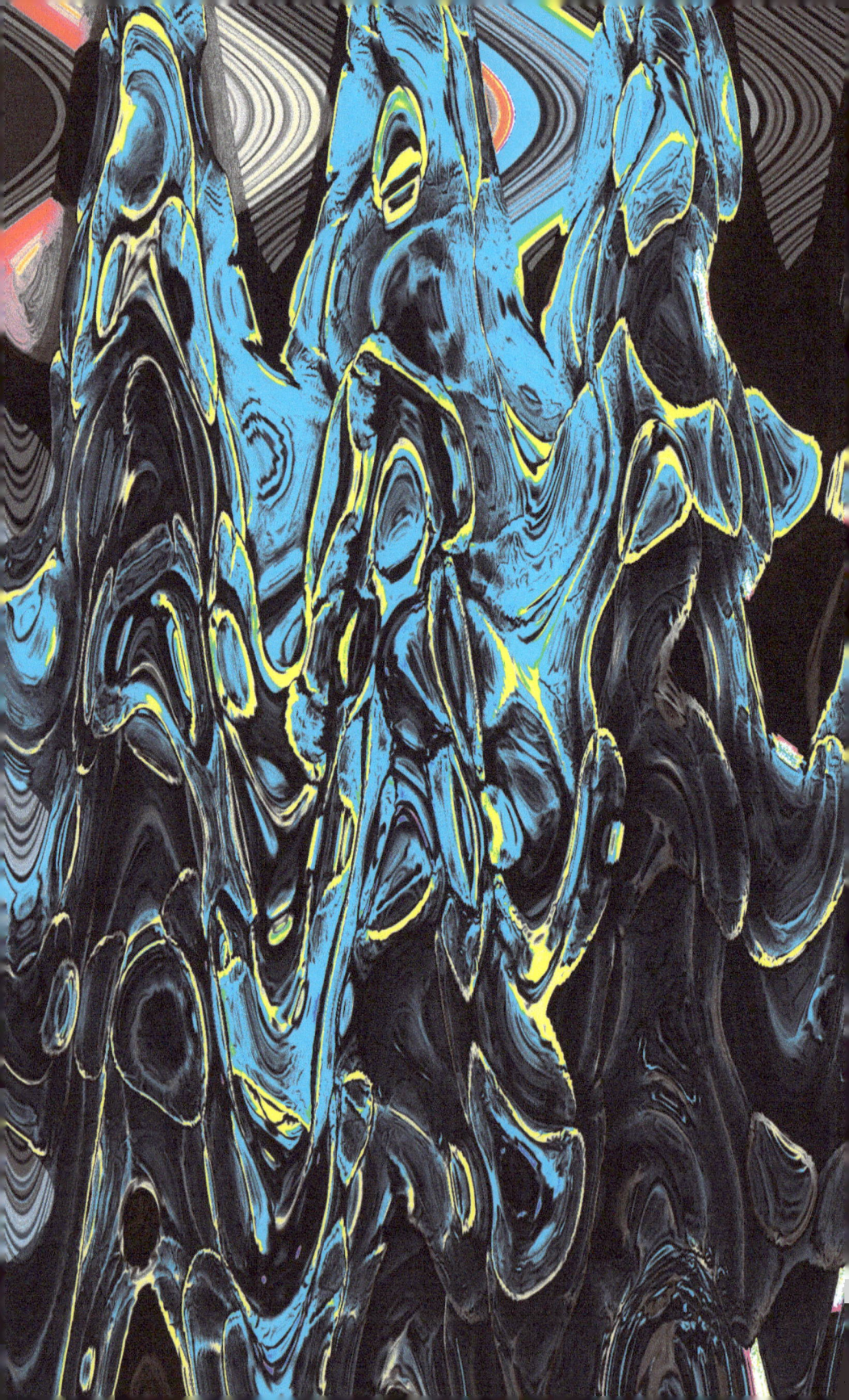

OKLAHOMA SHADOW

Blurred bodies in morning blue
The reflective shine of her soul
Empty shells
Open shot
Poured the petals in the rhyming sky
A naked frame of rosy wine
Threaded trash
A stand-alone crown
The commercial design of a broken heart
Molded and honest in the gloss of it's stand
Give me a smile
The sand in their eyes
A desperate climb for a delicate mind
The wrinkled waves of an isolated island
You're wrong
Crooked hands in the caves of their coats
The expanse of their lunar crimes
You're right
The dirty digs of a squandered soul
A powdered cake for the damned
Reversed the roles
The weary eyes
The brilliant shores wrapped in fire
Watching as the beauties roll by
Danger zones
Community press
The stinging pins of wind on your face

Roaming up and down as we speak
Sunken roses
The hurried street
The wild nightfall of splattered shrieks
The last-minute rush of the dead
Institutions of blood
The sobs in the swoon
The dawning build of puddled decay
Crashing in the arms of the fire
It could happen to you

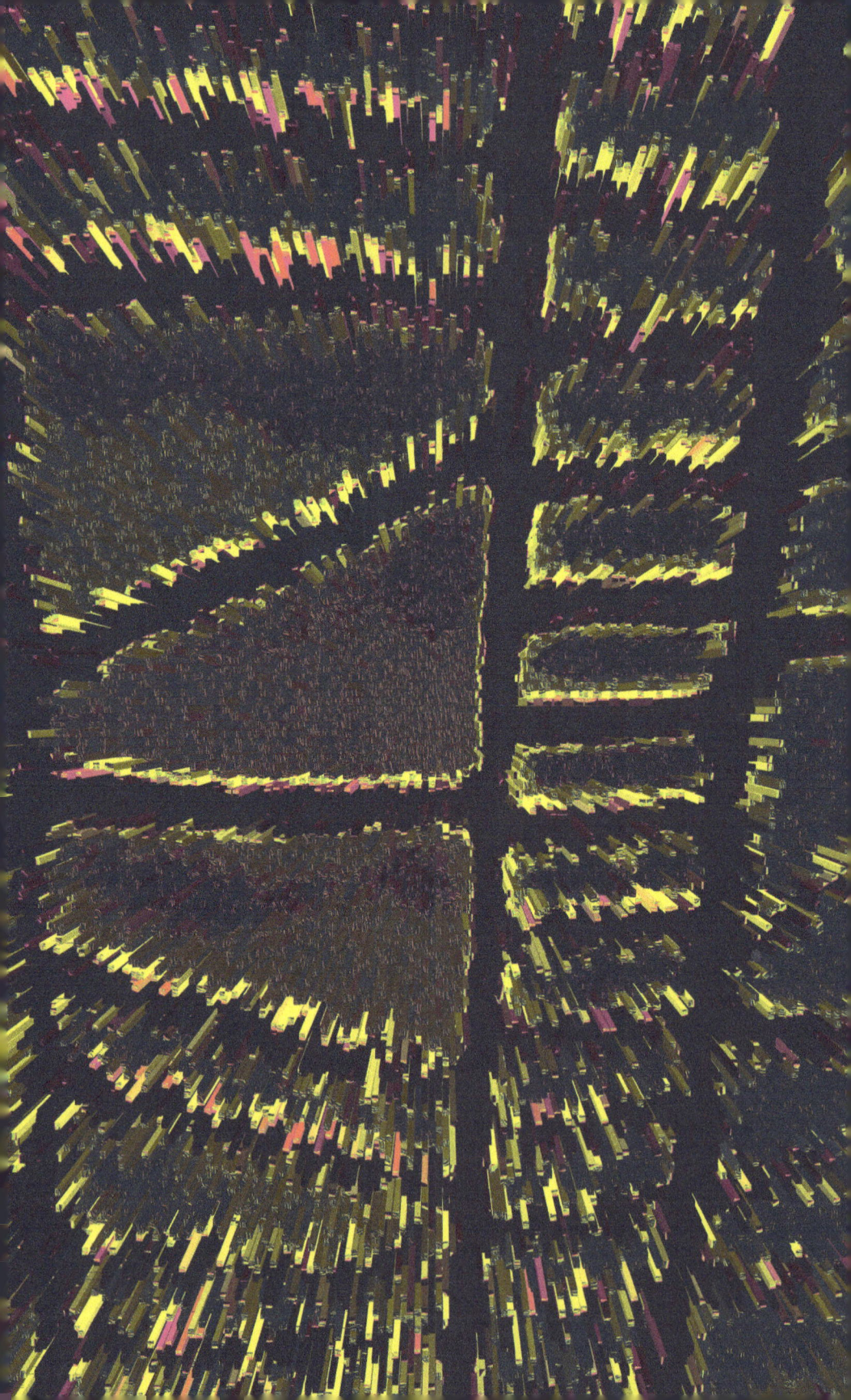

DARK COUNTRY

Scuffled raves
The crescent street
The labeled loads of assaulted souls
Fleeing to the core of the scene
Wounded tricks
The famous fluke
Tumbled floors on the silk of her shores
The rueful pursuit of their frantic climb
White-knuckle shrieks
The frontier flash
She'll run for the hills
A forbidden flow of bruised twilight in bloom
Intended to take flight
The scattered retreat of shapeless disguise
Singed their shot
The starchy smile
Glazed a gaze of unwanted parts
The shrunken mass of whittled shades
Flooded eyes
The brutal stretch
The cluttered view
A silent pact
Promising them to the moon and back
A faded rain pouring rambled & relaxed
The whispered night of teardrop assassins

HOTSY TOTSY

Stained in the rain
The lavish defeat
A studded hail of notes in the street
A starry facade of forgotten dreams
Flightless nights
The echoed eclipse
Hopeless floods of opposing worlds
The predicted rouse of new tidings
Wild streaks
The innocent bliss
The subtle scant of dancing thieves
Spilling their crests along the street
Saintly subversions
The vulnerable depths
Show-tune chateau of follies in blue
We'll ruffle them down the stream
Frequent flyers
A heart of cards
The royal whisk of elegant grade
Silent surfs
The shattered nerves
The steady stokes of steps in the dark
Engulfed among their corpses of clay

POPULAR RAINCOATS

Succumbing to their soundless laughs
The sequestered scratch in their step
Speedy pursuits
The collapse of their cries
A muddy double-deal of evening waves
The earthy stitch of their wasted shine
Damaged streaks
The rippled scheme
A fevered swim of rosy bloodshed
Pasted insane on the roof of their heads
Beauties in the bunk
The flop in their falls
A fainting flood of flattened affairs
A merriment in their match-box march
Sour notes
The indelible swoop
Ragged cascades of enveloped shock
The dismantled flock of spirits
Heated hearts
Thirsty dreams
Nestled under old tired eyes
Crushed their pennies on the under light drag

LUCKY ME

Come one, come all
The bludgeoned guise of vivid hope
Whittled wings
Flamboyant leaves
The shakes with no rhythm
The speech with no screams
Lucky me
Lucky you
All the mobs standing mute in the street
Vague by the side of pale tidings

Sunken worlds
The shiftless night
The whirling shine of shaded dreams
A punching bag stuffed with hearts
Sour drops
The empty lots
The shakes with no rhythm
The speech with no shrieks
Lucky you
Lucky me
The legs that quiver in the cells of their crates
Ditching bombs in the rain

Kiss and tell
A shooting star
The painted tears on open doors

Broad strokes
Abandoned fronts
The fervid strips throughout their face
You haven't changed a bit
The shakes with no rhythm
The speech with no screams
Lucky me
Lucky you
The weary eyes of a weeping willow
A powdered cake for the damned
Strolling on the floor

SUBLIMINAL MOVIES

The hasty cast of awakened hordes
A drop-down smudge in their smirk
Fatal faults
The subtle trace
The sacred verses wrapped in rain
A soaking frame of spattered stars
Faded bells
The final fall
The suspicious order of their poignant growth
The deflated spill of their soul
Trick of the trade
The abandoned rows of wandered souls
A promise on the prim
The classy reprise of their phantasmic shock
Passing their well-matched scraps on the ground
A staunch in their skip
The winning kicks
A faithful heart in ruined flakes
A switch-board source in their spine
Weary crews
The lucky divide
A lifeless line of sinking feuds
There comes a time where things must fade

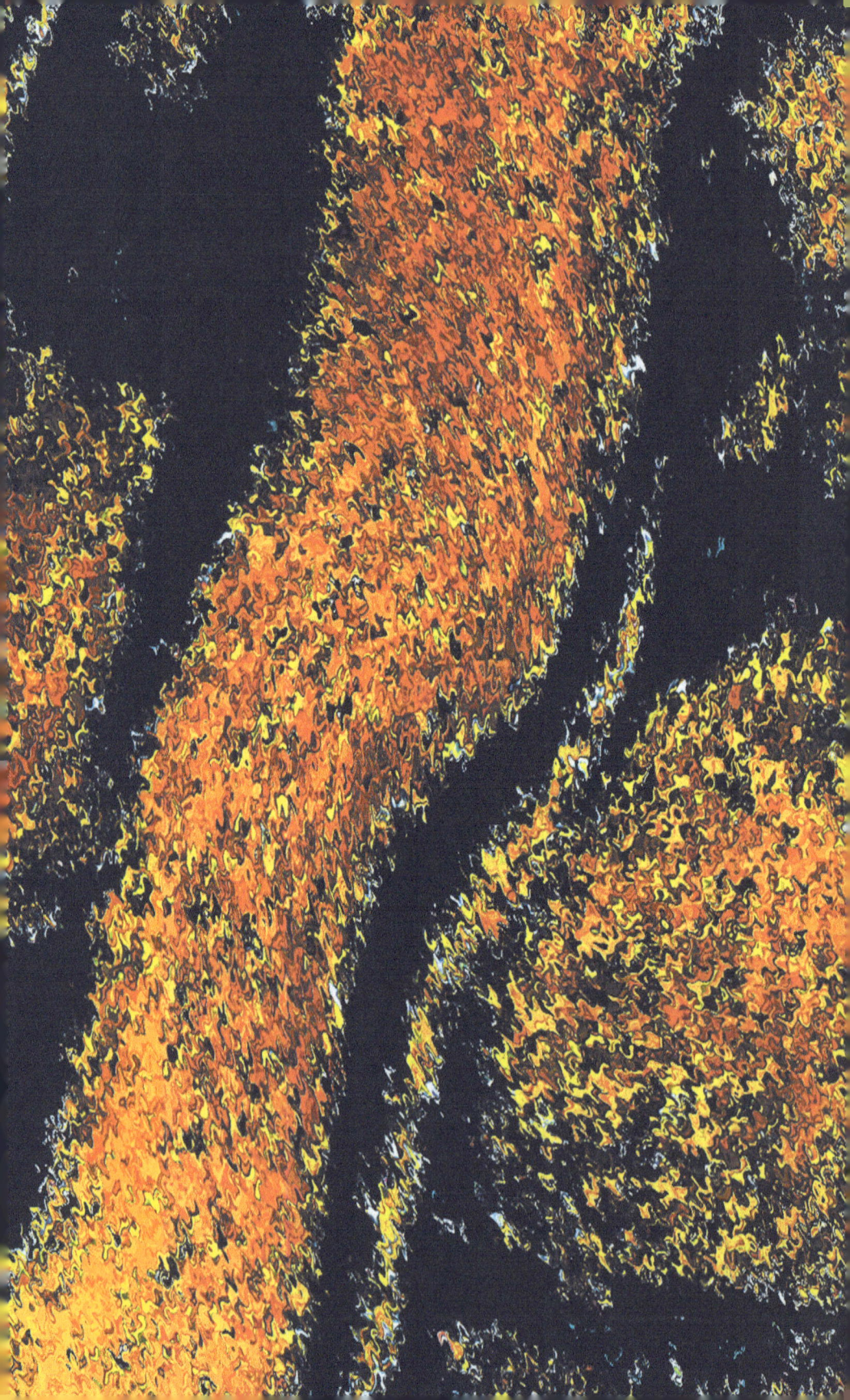

DARK TULIP

The automatic press
Shuffled isles in naked flamboyance
The wounded spread of their ruins
Par for the course
The predicted curse
A painted trail of fevered eyes
The disrupted troupe of old visions
Wasted tease
The ring of fire
The raptured charm of omnipotent flux
The schmuck with the overgrown mouth
Steer-born steed
The electric hoax
A flaming infusion of blended halves
The cross-hatched capture of thieves
Waded strides
An acquainted touch of exhausted dreams
The voluptuous wine
The excluded wish of first kisses
Bubbled-up verse
The nervous curse
An enclosed inversion of saints
A tangled ensemble in bloom
Drastic dash
The inflatable spread
Splashing their hands in pursuit of the news
The painted stir of new mornings

Dizzy deeds
The screeching streetcar treat
Bathed in bells at the broad stoke bash
The valiant raid of distracted clouds
What a day makes

FLAT MOUSE FRANKIE

A naked heart
The blood in their pockets
Slack and sullen in the will of their walk
The sloppy second-hand shake

Count your days
The aching arms
The roaring noise of blazing spines
Moaning from the dominance of the sky

Ears to the track
The mortal cluster
The dusty roads of buried dreams
Bludgeoned symbols in car-wrecked schemes
Pucker-up
The vicious flight
The first burst of rhyming frost
Leaking the lilacs along the street

Steady stokes
The charred departure
The marble strollers on the floor
In succession with the roadmap

A massive dugout
The circus stunts
You got skid marks on your face

A stacked cascade
The colorful gamble running silly in the rain
Oh, what a couple of old saucy dimes
Televised through kaleidoscopes

SEARSUCKER

The wonderment in their afflicted thrills
A buried splendor of painted plays
Rotted stacks
The romantic sway
The explosive scope of tumbling dreams
A barking plight of whispered veins
Gilded splash
The seasoned attack
An outward flash of their prospective heaven
The misfed measure of awakend impressions
Nervous breeds
The missile effect
The mortal pour of their shatterted dreams
An impossible flock of animated streets
The run-rush string of rebellion
Sordid planes
The pumped-up dud
The rapid growth of glorified mornings
A swill of swallowed encryptions
Gaping bonds
The honorable press
Clipped their wings in filtered exhibits
The bandit with the suspended eyes
Severed stops
The meticulous catch
Counting cards
The perpetual glance

A wanted stooge running loose in the sun
Ghostly tracks
The tight-rope sketch
The doll with the crimson lipstick

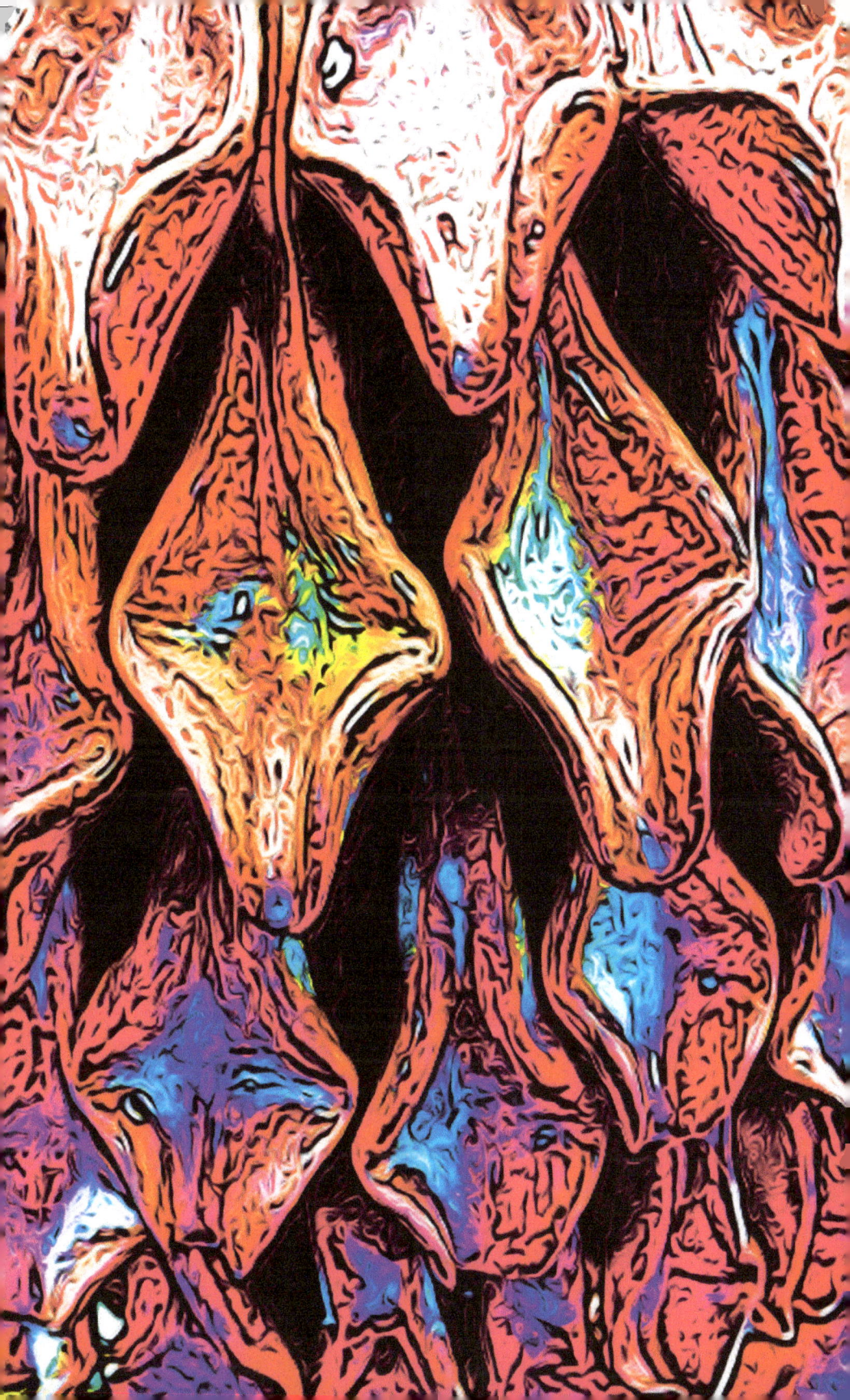

JUNIOR JOEY

The guarded disguise of divided light
The roll-around scent of sweet wonders
Crowded muse
The autonomous ruse
The lyrical scorch of tainted infernos
A beguiled badge of idols in the trench
Wanted snuffs
The extended crush
The mortal clutch of fallen depths
Scattered wrecks
The moveable catch
The subtle sweep of shuffled stars
The enamored splash of her twirl
Slow retreat
The ambushed swing
An enduring sweep of public crimes
A wounded twitch of silent cries
Twisted scenes
The filthy switch
The immaculate press
A flashback express
An unmatched patch of overgrown skies
The snow-fallen scope of their animated minds
Blank space
A stationary taste
The shuffled splurge of spoiled wine
A wandered script of severed skies

The dystopian taste of her lips
A forgotten fix
A scruffy crowd of silenced streets
The lashing splash of secluded saints
An improbable break for the meek
Tumbled tastes
A folly cause
Descended swarms
The culminated prop
An acquainted state of chaotic shock
The sinful cast of the settled and sick
Sunken dreams
The monetary beast
A classy cast of juggled spills
The ravenous switch of lamented calls
Itchy grit
The motivated melt
The concentrated score of cherished waves
A wasted stay of eternal impressions

FEMME FATALE

Saintly revisions
The grounded pulse upon their lying wait
The lonely stampede of their vulnerable fate
A crushing end to a whistful whim
A willowed cast of schmucks in the night
Saviors son
Battanical crest
The laughing stint of studded skies
Painful stings of arrested goodboyes
At what cost?
Out in the blue
At what risk?
Can you see them dropping
All the murky masts of embedded names
Scultpted falls of frivilous wakes
What about the ___
A trailing pool of depleted streets
Watchful postures of collided grasps
Rippled roads
The fragmented dance
An assembled score of pouring rain
The afflicted barrage of carnage on your hands
And all we can do is cry
Gutted tears
An assassinated step
The gushing blush of arrested lips
Raging coutures of demolished hips

And all we can do is weep
Vicious flaunt
The crooked design
The blinding light of submersive collapse
Screaming in sin, who really gives a crap?
And all we can do is wail
External demands
The rougish retreat
A hazy paste of appointed shrines
The shredded flock of elementary talk
And all we can do is whine
Silent crimes
The spontaneous oath
The fleeting remains of their beating hearts
A weary retreat of the sick and the old
And all we can do is moan
Gratuitious catch
The frivolus flight
A marveled swell of deserted sounds
The deflated game of their wounded smiles
And all we can do is laugh

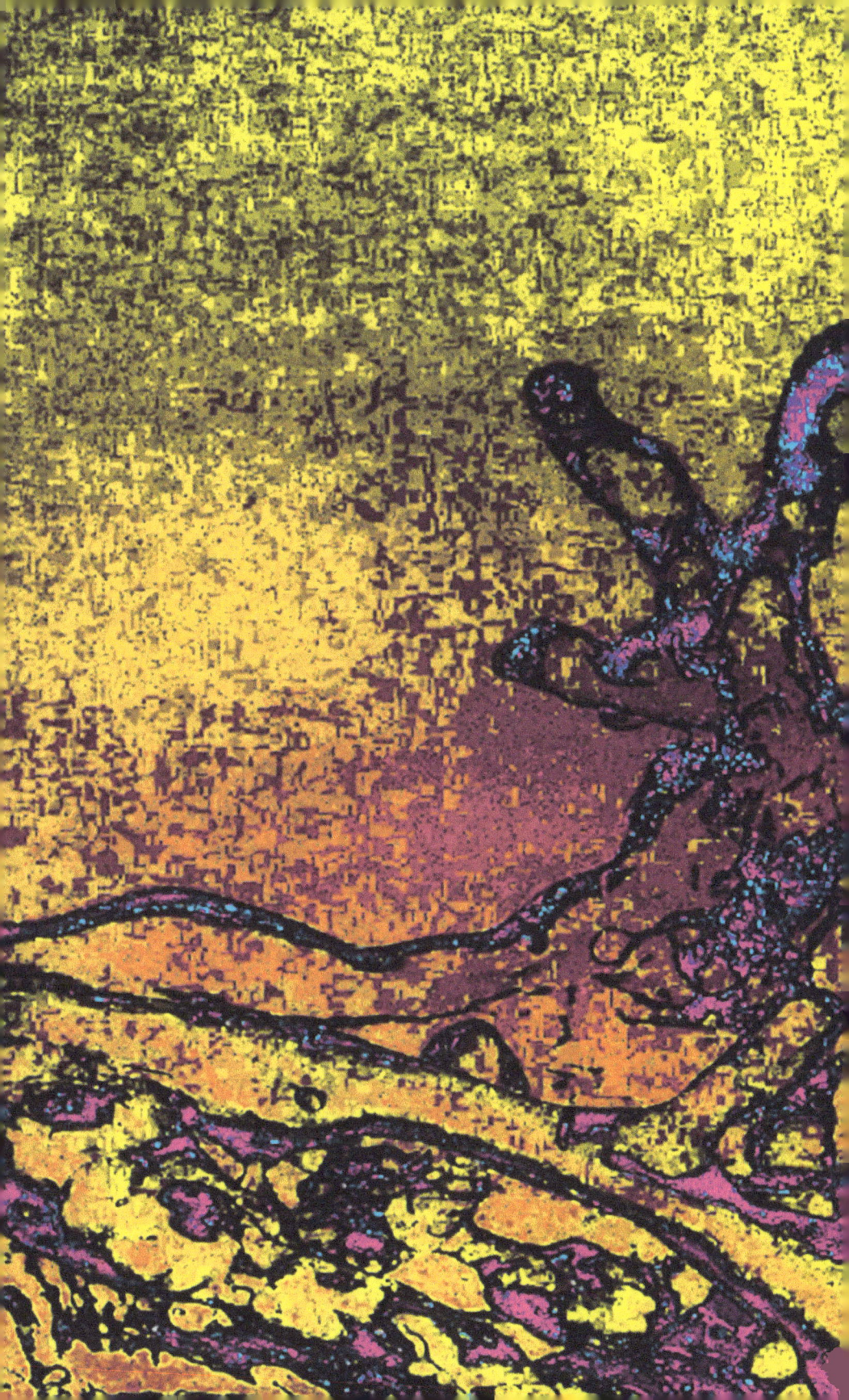

MAIN LINE SPINE

A moseyed trail of tribal scripts
The sequenced sketch of splashing hands
The cherished march
A psychic start
A reflection of their sad affairs

Splendid source
The anxious vote
An awakened sense of soluble fronts
The cautioned pitch of tender notes

Sweet to taste
The final match
Classy dash
A dispatched dance
A one-way trick in their harmonious plans
The day-to-day encounters of salvation

Sunken heads
The solid marks
A sacrificial state of their luxurious match
The resistors at the table
What's your name?
A tortured race
An electric thirst of experienced speech
The silent send-off of flaming streets
Do you feel them running through the windows?

SHEIKI GARDEN

The wistful spill of their soulful screams
A suspended parade of colorful shades
Beaten paths
The blissful stir
An anchored enclave of inflatable skies
The impacted lapse of their cries
Sunken masts
The thrashing pun
A sheltered exclaim of afflicted grief
The offensive batch of ascended thieves
Double dose
The afflicted wave
Where do you rest your dead?
A despondent taste of her cradled kiss
The mishandled swipe of soaring fists
Ruddy breaks
The idol express
Calling cards
The misguided stage
Swarmed their hands with the sight of the blast
The peaceful patch of their outlandish source
Wonder what a sight it must be?
The whispered wish of expired thoughts
Caressing up and down the street
Shielded sounds
The eruptive sketch
A broken return aimed at the road

The ambushed crush of her flailing dress

BAROLLA

The innocent play of invented laughs
A resemblance in their stammered route
Hustled scuffs
The conquered class
The arduous track of their cavernous front
A careless catch of fallen stars
Smooth expiry
The conscious wit
A strained pain in their impassive face
The disappearing piece of swarming crowns
Flavored strips
A nasty take
Stutter struck
The mummified troupe
A revolving rain of clouded sparks
The enamored clash of her mane
Vague proposals
The declarations in the dark
The hungry hordes
A conscious catch of damaged roots
The roguish entrenchment of skins
Combative costs
The hapless reach
The swindled wreck of melting hands
A hallmark of their reckless hearts
Huddled press
A haggard prop of shuttled steps

Bitter doves
The immortal lure of their fantastic swell
A fielded fjords of polyester visions
The persistent weight of their worries
An immortal lure of their fantastic swell

THE BALLAD OF JACK JENCH

The somber spill of singing guards
A hanging slew of ruinous news
Chaotic scrolls
The twisted scrawl
A wilted thrust of reclusive souls
The mark of an armored muse
For the ballad of Jack Jench

Bartered parts
The half-hearted charm
A scenic vulgarity of blushing skies
The woven grapple of spinning eyes
Can you hear them bouncing off the streets?
Veiled surprise
A frightful truth
A crowded scope of layered spills
The luscious crush of flooded kicks
For the ballad of Jack Jench

Plastered breaks
The functioned drunk
Twisted ends
An isolated blunt
The rotten trail of shambled skirts
Knocking them over where it hurts
For the ballad of Jack Jench

A hazy spread of whistled drafts
Crushed contempt
The silent attempt
The curly clod of unspoken locks
An impassioned cleanse of neglected faults
For the ballad of Jack Jench

The distorted tangle of streets
Silted sands
The hopeless flight
The equivocal catch of knitted skies
Flimsy hymns
An effervescent rose
The pulsing invasion of sprinted phrases
A one-way punch to the nose
To the ballad of Jack Jench

CAN YOU SEE THE MOON OVER SOHO?

Can you see the moon over Soho?
And the flimsy streets turn old
They were my friends, and then they went away

The authentic sketch of playful games
And the boulevards paved with gold
Can you see the moon over Soho?

Over the moon, the indelible sway
Of shifting seas that roll and roll
They were my friends, and then they went away

Her lady-like pose, the haunting domain
The blinded shine of crimes untold
Can you see the moon over Soho?

Top of the deck, the autonomous reign
And the ravaged tales soon foretold
They were my friends, and then they went away
Can you see the moon over Soho?

WHEN I MET OBJECT X

The arrested channel of scribbled flocks
A bottomless shot of lucid thoughts
Silent caress
The blank canvas
A layered plight of snowy-white stars
The humored blotch of bloody scars
Can we yearn for them to be safe?
Runny rows
The immaculate crest
The painted frame of exhausted stacks
A tactful stretch of dusty tracks
Collective catch
The sleuth in their arms
A belligerent draught of accented skies
The grandiose stroke of sprawling knives
Can we yearn for them to thrive?
Pistol pop
Unrivaled delight
The elevation of their veiny hands
An inordinate slump of their juggling heads
Careless escape
The beaten route
Can we yearn for them to be free?
The intangible muse of sunken ships
The dying light of cascading tricks
Reclusive wish
A blissful tryst

The roses unfurled around their beds
A whittled stitch of stricken waves
Can we yearn for them to run?
Urban panorama
The bludgeoned trauma
A bouquet of beauties engulfed in the trench
The fruitless devise of their salty revenge
A baptized remise of pleated legs
The rushing cluster engulfed in the sand
Do we yearn for them to be dead?

CITADELLA...

A wistful stitch of vibrant skies
See the vacant slot of blocks that trail
Captured bliss
The improbable spell
An imprisoned glimpse of thrashing waves
The surrounding scenes of banished streets
Spelled
C
I
T
A
D
E
L
L
A mismatched patch of hoarded shells
Hear the haunted spell of shattered bells
Roaring scores
The romantic swing
A vague reclaim of faded moons
Winking through their steepled rooms
Spelled
C
I
T
A
D

E
L
L

An enchanted mess of broken glass
The embodied blend of buried hands
Whispered chants
An altered pursuit
The ballistic twist of silent lights
Surrounded by the sounds of the night
Spelled

C
I
T
A
D
E
L
L

An anchored mast of stranded stars
The rosaceous cast of vacant plots
Tender notes
The ravenous quote
A moseyed trail of collected
The strangled drop of flooded caves
Spelled

C
I
T
A
D
E

L
L
A

POKERFACE

Auspicious waves of ecstatic wings
The suspended view of their damaged muse
Fringed delight
The divided course
A feathered cascade of spangled crusades
The lauded trail of trivial games
Ragged casts
The dreadful crux
Wrapped with luck
The sputtered splash of furious waves
A misguided stream of restless flames
Enchanted mess
The impulsive drop
The palatial prop of divided crowds
A midnight shroud of rambling sounds
Can you see them stalking the streets?
Messy pause
The forgotten stir
Vicious flaunt
The zestful tinge of gallant storms
Lovely crush
The melodic caress of tangled lights
An ejected stretch of peaceful nights
Can you see them on the other side?
Pleasure & pain
The illustrious beat

A rippled strip of their bloodless eclipse
The nauseous thrall in their voiceless relief
Can you see them dancing in the streets?
Steady flow
The matchless quill of deleted scenes
Departed forms
The spattered batch of tainted blood
The dissembled string of coruscant dreams
Tasteless facade
A majestic phrase
Can you see them swarming in the streets?

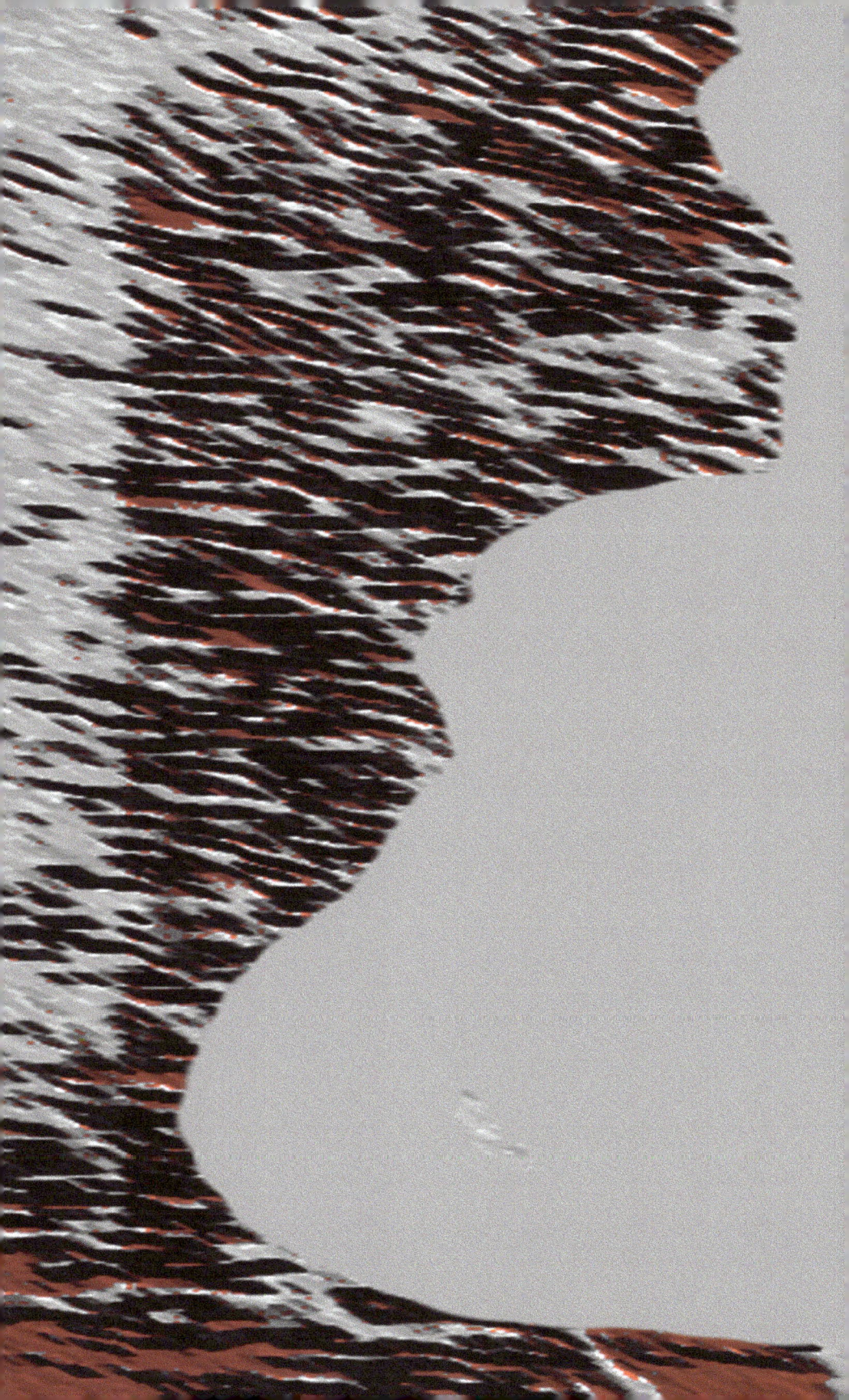

THE VOICE BEHIND THE VERSE

Tristan Buttigieg is a passionate poet, musician, singer-song-writer, and artist. His debut poetry collection, Have Nine Lives, explored the complexities of the human experience. In his follow-up collection, Pearlesque, Buttigieg delves deeper into themes of love, hope, loss, resilience, transformation, and self-discovery. With lyrical verses that blend beauty and raw emotion, Pearlesque invites readers on a journey of reflection and healing.

As a multifaceted artist, Buttigieg's work spans poetry, music, and visual art, reflecting his belief in the transformative power of creative expression. Central to his vision is the idea that art is open to interpretation, encouraging readers to bring their unique perspectives to his work.

Published by Cykxbooks, Pearlesque marks an exciting evolution in Buttigieg's literary and artistic journey, offering a deeper and more nuanced exploration of the human condition. When not writing, he enjoys creating music, art, and exploring how literature and the arts connect and heal people.

"You feel the words rather than just read them. They're warm, soft, chilling, violent, scary, beautiful, and a million other things. Poetry well done."
— Amazon Review

"Perfectly captures the raw essence of existence, while hinting at the complexities and contradictions of life."
— Amazon Review

"A vivid tapestry of imagery and emotion. Tristan's work creates a hauntingly beautiful atmosphere. Each line evokes a sense of nostalgia and reflection, painting a picture of life's fleeting moments and the inevitable passage of time."
— Instagram Review

Discover More Of The Author's Work:

Explore the world of Tristan Buttigieg's poetry with Have Nine Lives, his debut collection that takes you on an emotional journey through themes of love, loss, and the human experience.

Have Nine Lives is available now—order your copy and dive into a beautifully crafted collection that will captivate and inspire.
Stay updated on future projects and creative content, by visiti-following on social media.

Join The Creative Community:

Stay connected and be the first to know about new releases, exclusive updates, and behind-the-scenes insights into the creative process.

Instagram: @officialtristanbuttigieg
Twitter: @TristanAJB
Facebook: @TristanButtigieg
YouTube: Tristan Buttigieg